Water Awarenes

A parent's guide to teaching TODDLERS water safety & how to enjoy the water

Part of the Water Awareness Series
By AlyT

Format: Jonny Hossain
Editing: Jessica Raymond
Illustrator: Emets Anna Alekseevna
First printing: 2022

Disclaimer
While we draw on our own prior professional expertise and background in the area of teaching learn to swim, by purchasing and reading our products you acknowledge that we have produced this book for informational and educational purposes only. You alone are solely responsible and take full responsibility for your own well-being as well as the health, lives and well-being of your family and children in your care.

www.BornToSwim.com.au
SwimMechanics@yahoo.com
Other books by this Author:
Water Awareness Newborns
Water Awareness Babies
Learn to Swim the Australian Way Level 1 – The Foundations
Learn to Swim the Australian Way Level 2 – The Basics
Learn to Swim the Australian Way Level 3 – Intermediate
Learn to Swim the Australian Way Level 4 – Advanced

"Before I spoke a word,
You were singing over me...
Before I took a breath,
You breathed Your life in me..."

Reckless Love, Cory Asbury

SAFETY FIRST!

SUPERVISE

Babies, toddlers and children **ALWAYS** require strict and constant supervision in and around water.
When a child loves water but does not have basic water safety skills, the risk of drowning increases.
NEVER LEAVE children unattended, as drowning can occur in very shallow water (wading pools, fishponds, buckets, toilets, eskies, bathtubs etc.).
It is important you turn off & tune out all distractions and give your kids your **FULL ATTENTION** when they are around water.
Regardless of age and ability, **NO CHILD OR PERSON IS DROWN PROOF**

SAFETY PLAN

We recommend every family has a **WATER SAFETY PLAN** - a plan provides LAYERS OF PROTECTION you can add to keep your family safer around water. Supervision, barriers, temptations & access to all forms of water (pools, water tanks, septic tanks, lakes, dams etc.), **LEARNING CPR** and knowing **EMERGENCY SERVICE NUMBERS** should all form part of your plan.

SUBMERSIONS

Forced submersions, by **THROWING AND DUNKING** a child, can frighten them resulting in unwanted ingestion of water and an aversion to water.
Be very conscious of how much water your child ingests during their lesson, as excessive ingesting of water can cause water intoxication and poses a very serious health risk. For more information, search: **HYPONATREMIA.**

SLIPPING HAZARDS

Be mindful of slippery surfaces and tripping hazards when around water. Encourage children to always walk and never run, wrestle or play in wet areas.
At the conclusion of lessons, make use of handrails, stairs, ladders etc. Encourage young children to exit the water carefully and only with your permission.

STAY WARM

Check the water temperature before commencing your aquatic lessons. Water temperature that is too cold will result in children becoming cold and not enjoying their lessons. **THINK AHEAD** by having warm towels close by.
Lesson duration should not exceed 30mins. Always aim to finish the lesson before children show signs of hunger, tiredness or become unsettled.

SUPPORT YOUR TODDLER

Toddlers should be properly supported whilst in water to prevent swallowing excessive amounts of water and becoming unbalanced.

AN UNBALANCED TODDLER WILL BECOME UNCOMFORTABLE AND SHOW SIGNS OF DISTRESS. Please read our guide to aquatic holds.

Before we begin...

G'day Grommies & Rugrats

Welcome to the third and final book of our Water Awareness Series for Infants. Whether you're new to our guides or have been following along with each book, Water Awareness for Toddlers has been written to expand your water awareness education and teach water safety skills to pre-schoolers as a bridge between Parent & Baby classes and their first structured Learn-To-Swim class.

During your toddler's class, we encourage the use of swim equipment such as kickboards, sink toys, plastic mirrors, pool noodles, etc. These items all have a purpose and should only be used at the appropriate time during the lesson. We discourage the use of floatation garments/accessories and goggles during classes because an overreliance on either can negatively affect and slow down your toddler's skill acquisition. We want our little ones to learn to be comfortable getting water in their eyes, ears and nose, and to learn to float using their muscles, breath and body positioning so they can experience how to balance and stay buoyant. Best to put these items aside for playtime or use after their classes have finished.

Last of all... As most parents would already know, toddlers (18mths – 36mths) can be very insistent and not always the most agreeable little people at times. This age group is also known for either their over-enthusiastic (often dangerous) curiosity of water OR their ingrained fear and dislike of water. Keeping this in mind, let's remember to maintain structure, reinforce the safety rules, limit distractions and stay focused.

Let's aim for every lesson to be memorable by making it fun and full of positive encouragement so we can all be safer around water - Learn what you don't know, reinforce correctly what you do know and don't let your toddler regress by taking too much time off between lessons.

Ready to dive in? Let's get wet!!

Yours swimmingly,
Aly T

Ps, it's ok to teach your toddler to blow bubbles on the surface of the water, but we're still holding our breath for buoyancy with this age group until we enter our Learn To Swim classes after 36 months; so for now avoid asking your toddler to blow bubbles when submerging their face.

AlyT

Aquatic Holds

How you hold an infant during their swimming lessons has a huge impact on their comfort and learning experience. Well-intentioned adults who use improper or clumsy holds during a swim class can unwittingly impede the learning process by frustrating or upsetting their young student swimmers. All the activities in our guide are accompanied by colourful illustrations of suggested holds and body positions to use during your lessons.
We can't stress enough the importance of being mindful of holding children correctly when in the water.

Remember to always stay within arm's reach of your toddler, because unlike babies who need to be constantly held, toddlers can be fiercely independent and insist on doing things 'by themselves'. When you are holding them, hold them lightly to allow them to feel and experience their buoyancy and always ensure they are well balanced.

Legs curling up behind them, arching backs, forming a 'v' with their body, crying, coughing/gagging and grabbing at your hands are clear indicators your little one is unbalanced, frightened, uncomfortable or swallowing/snorting water. Sometimes, water can tickle little ears or run into their eyes and cause discomfort; over time, with a little reassurance, they will adjust.

For toddlers, we encourage underarm holds around the armpits and shoulders for most of the water activities when teaching back floats, front floats, kickboard holds, vertical and horizontal turns. Holding toddlers under the armpits and around the shoulders gives them a sense of independence to freely splash, wriggle and feel their buoyancy whilst also giving them a sense of security knowing they are being safely held by a trustworthy adult.

Never let go, dunk or throw a child in the water unless they specifically ask you to. One bad water experience can cause a lifetime of harm to their aquatic learning journey.

For activities that require young ones to lay on their back, we encourage standing behind the little swimmer with your hands supporting them by the shoulders whilst maintaining constant eye contact.

Enter Safely

Entering water safely is one of the most important skills you can teach your toddler. Instil in them the water safety rules right from the start:

- they are not to enter or play with water without permission or invitation from a responsible adult,
- to always stay within arm's reach of an adult, and
- to remain within sight when they are in and around water.

Toddlers are known for their curiosity, so when around any type of water explain to them using clear, concise age-appropriate language why it is important to stay close and ask for permission before going to play. By doing so, they will better understand and learn to respect the water.

Before entering the water, make sure any equipment you intend to use during the lesson is close by and easy for you to access.

As you wade into the water, let your tot know if there are any slippery surfaces and what could happen if they run and trip or do not hold your hand and handrails etc. Show them where the water is too deep or unsafe and most importantly, explain to them to stay close to you in case they need your help.

Your toddler can easily lose balance and topple over during the early stages of learning to wade and walk in water. They will need your assistance to stay upright, sit and recover to a standing position until they can balance on their feet unassisted. Encourage them to use their arms to balance and to walk slowly and carefully; staying within arm's reach.

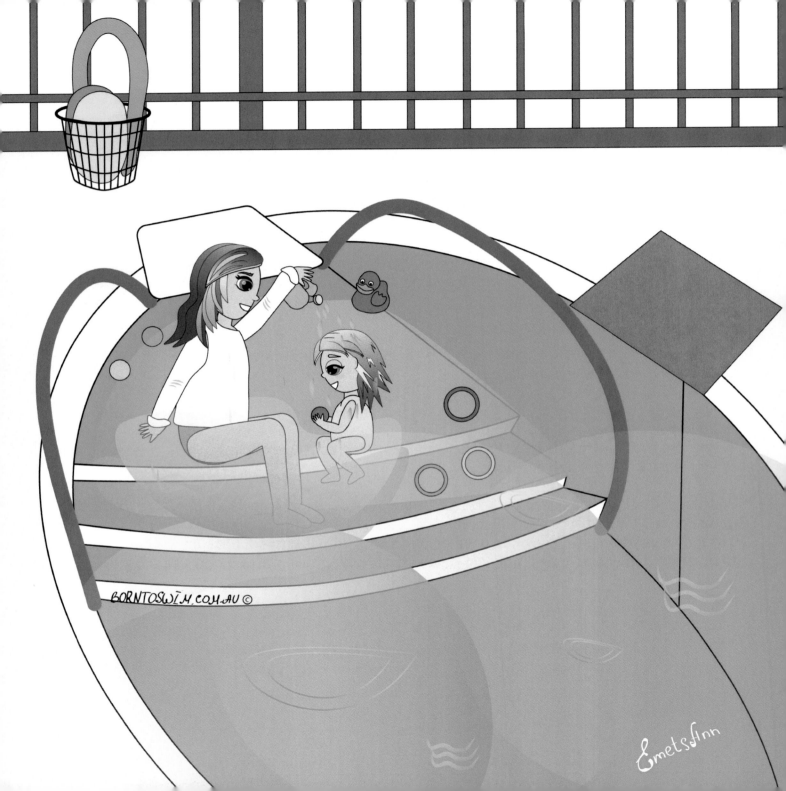

Explore and Condition

Exploration through shallow water play is an important facet of water education for toddlers, especially for the hesitant or fearful toddler. By playing and exploring the properties of water, they learn about its texture and how it moves - like the effect their movements can have on it and the effects water can have on them.

Shallow water play is also an excellent environment to build independence and realise their own limitations. Under strict supervision, they'll learn about buoyancy, get a 'feel for the water' and discover which teaching toys float and which one's sink. They'll also learn about shallow and deep areas of the water environment which is important for them to learn where they can play safely and where they will need your assistance.

When your toddler is relaxed and comfortable playing and exploring the water, it is also the perfect opportunity to introduce breath control through Conditioning.

Conditioning teaches your little one to hold their breath on cue when water touches their face. It also prepares them for holding onto their breath when going underwater. Conditioning is always practiced using a three-part verbal cue:
the child's name – ready – go!

Say 'their name' to get their attention, 'ready' to encourage them to take in a breath and hold it, and on 'go' gently sprinkle or pour water, using items such as - small watering cans, cups, the sprinkler setting of a hose, waterfalls, water fountains etc. over their face.

Crocodiles

Learning to 'Crocodile' creates body awareness by teaching your toddler to balance in the water with their legs and arms outstretched while maintaining a horizontal body position.

To Crocodile, encourage your little one to lay flat in shallow water and float their legs up behind them with their feet and toes pointed, and only their heels breaking the surface of the water. This is the Crocodile tail.

To move through the shallow water, encourage them to use long, slow arm extensions to reach and pull themselves along.

If not ready to submerge their full face, have them hold their breath and leave only their eyes out of the water as they stalk their sink toys and follow you through the water like a crocodile.

Kicking

The correct kicking technique does not come naturally without lots of repetitive practice. A welltaught and often practiced kick will ensure your toddler gets strong, propulsion from their legs and feet, making learning to swim a whole lot easier for them.

To teach your toddler to kick, sit in shallow water with your legs extended and floating straight out in front of you, keeping your toes and feet pointed away from you.

Kick slowly by raising and lowering each leg under the water, like a pair of scissors, letting only the top of your foot break the surface as you create lots of bubbles with your toes and feet. Encourage your toddler to mimic your kicking action as they sit beside you or on your lap with their legs extended over your legs and kick along with you.

To help guide their kick, place your hands under their knees with thumbs just below the kneecap and kick their legs for them. Alternate between letting them kick assisted and unassisted.

When kicking on their belly, lay your toddler on their stomach in shallow water to limit the depth of their kick. Have your little one kick fast little kicks by pointing their toes with long straight legs.

Their feet should just break the surface, and if they are bending their knees too much, reach over and assist by placing your hands under their kneecaps and your thumbs over their calves to make lots of fast little kicks as you count to ten.

BORNTOSWIM.COM.AU ©

Emetsfinn

Front floats

Floating face down weightlessly on their belly teaches your toddler to relax, feel their own buoyancy, balance & stabilise and develop breath control.

To float, start by practicing in very shallow water. Have your toddler lay flat in the water, while you lean in to hold them gently by the shoulders. Instruct them to take in a big breath and hold it using the Conditioning cue.

On 'go!' have them place their entire face into the water, pull them gently towards you and hold them very still as you count from a second or two up to the count of 5 or 10 whilst they float and hold their breath. Encourage them to spread out their arms and legs until they look like a starfish or an aeroplane floating on the surface of the water. Over time, incrementally lessen the support of your hands until they can front float, with their face in the water, without your assistance.

Water-shy toddlers can also practice their front floats by laying flat, holding their breath and dipping just their chins into the water as you hold them and count.

When your tot can front float without your assistance, advance to teaching them to float face down whilst holding a kickboard. Holding the kickboard will enable them to learn to float and balance with their arms extended out front.

We encourage all little swimmers to hold the kickboard using the Crocodile Hold – eyes looking down, elbows are locked with arms kept straight and shoulder distance apart, fingers on top of the kickboard and thumbs underneath to keep a firm grip.

Once they can front float with a kickboard in the correct position, we can encourage them to start kicking and gliding across short distances whilst maintaining the horizontal body position and holding the kickboard.

Back floats

The back float is an essential water safety skill that should be learnt in case of an accidental fall into the water and a staple for teaching balance and buoyancy on the back.

To back float, have your toddler lay on their back in calm, shallow water with their head cradled in your lap. Support their head with your hands or gently hold them by the shoulders as you talk and maintain eye contact. Remind them to relax and keep their ears and toes under the water whilst laying flat with arms and legs stretched wide like a starfish or feet together like a sharp pencil, as you count to ten and they float.

If uncomfortable laying on their back, distract them with a toy, songs and reassurance. Alternatively, rest the back of their head against your chest and gradually lower them into the water away from your body whilst still holding their shoulders.

A Teddy Bear Hug of a kickboard can also increase your toddler's confidence and put them into the correct body position for back floating and learning to kick on their back. Place the board under their chin pressed against their stomach and hold it in place by giving it a firm hug.

When kicking on their back, encourage your little swimmer to keep their ears under, hug the kickboard close to their chest and to kick small baby kicks, this will ensure they do not become unbalanced or splash water on their face.

To return to a standing position from the back float, instruct your toddler to sit up by lifting their head and getting them to look at their feet whilst also spreading their arms wide to balance as they plant their feet on the ground and stand back up.

Submerging

Submerging the face whilst holding their breath will greatly increase your toddler's fun and skill acquisition, but they must be ready and well prepared through consistent Conditioning before attempting submersions. A poorly timed or surprise submersion can cause a curious toddler to become a fearful learner.

For the timid toddler who is not ready to submerge, going under the water can be a huge hurdle. They must be given lots of opportunities to relax and play in the water. Sometimes letting them watch other children of similar age playing and ducking under the water is enough for them to want to try it for themselves.

Alternatively, encourage your tot to incrementally submerge parts of their face and body until they are ready to submerge their whole face. Start with getting their shoulders under, wetting one ear at a time as they listen to the water, and lowering themselves into the water until their chin and lips are under.

Most times, submerging is a game of patience and gentle persistence; never use force or shaming but do look for fun toys and games they can play to slowly desensitise their fear and increase their willingness to go fully under the water. Hold your toddler's hand as they self-submerge or partially submerge to retrieve items and chicken peck their faces into the water until they want to do it on their own.

Once a toddler can successfully submerge a new world of confidence and exploration will begin, we can reintroduce the front floats, encourage submerging for sink toys, teach free floats and so much more.

To free float, your tot simply self-submerges from one area, pushes off with their feet and floats horizontally to an adult or to the side of the pool.

Reach and Paddle

Reaching and paddling teaches your toddler to move through the water with their arms extended out in front of them for balance and to use an effective arm propulsion to pull and push the water.

To teach your toddler to paddle the water, we first show them how to 'feel the water' by holding their wrists and helping them move the water with their hands to feel its pressure.

We teach our tots to reach and paddle by extending each arm forwards under the water then bending the elbow to push the water behind them with their hands.
NOTE: After each push of the water, the arm returns to full extension via under the water not over the surface.

Alternate between assisting your little one to reach and paddle by moving their arms for them as they sit on your lap and holding them on your knee as you walk in deeper water.

To further advance their paddling skills have your toddler self-submerge, free float and paddle out to you. Keep the distance they need to travel to a minimum, no more than a meter or two, so they don't run out of breath or start to struggle.

Before you return them to the shallow step or side of the pool, reinforce the reach and paddling technique by assisting them again on your lap. You can support yourself by sitting them on your raised knee as you hold and guide their wrists. Then send them back encouraging them to 'Reach & Paddle!', 'Reach & Paddle!'.

Once your tot has mastered reaching and paddling without your assistance, encourage them to add small kicks as they independently propel themselves through the water.

Swim Arounds

As your toddler becomes more confident in the water, we want to encourage independence and water safety as much as possible. Swim arounds will teach your tot to explore and respect deeper water, return themselves to safety, self-submerge and move through the water, at a safe distance from you, without assistance.

Swim arounds are a combination of the skills your toddler has already learnt (crocodiling, submerging, breath holding, kicking and reaching & paddling).

To perform a swim around, sit on a shallow submerged step and encourage your little swimmer to circle you by alternating between a slow Crocodile crawl across the shallow water behind you and kicking and paddling through the deeper water out in front of you whilst maintaining a horizontal body position.

Assist them when necessary, by holding their hand or guiding them in a semi-circle through the deeper water by holding them under the arms as they pass by you. As their confidence and propulsive skills grow, encourage independent Swim Arounds.

Vertical Turns

Vertical turns will teach and reinforce returning to a safe place after entering the water. They are essential when learning survival swimming in the event of an accidental fall into the water.

Vertical Turns should be taught in 3 stages:
- how to jump in safely,
- how to change direction and turn vertically in the water, and
- how to return to the wall.

When jumping into the water we want to instil safe water practices like waiting for permission and checking to see if it is safe before jumping in. Rather than encouraging your toddler to jump into your arms, which can sometimes result in an injury, we should instead guide our tots into the water away from the edge, on cue, by holding their hand and having them land beside us so we can assist them, or they can grasp onto us easily.

To teach the assisted Vertical Turns, we hold our little one under the armpits and practice half turns and full turns whilst they are submerged. Playing a game of Peek-A-Boo as you spin them under the water will make the turns fun and enjoyable.

Once your toddler can turn without your assistance, practice the Vertical Turns near the shallow steps and encourage them to turn themselves under the water and to reach and paddle back to the submerged step moving away from you.

Once each stage has been practiced individually, we can start practicing Vertical Turns by jumping into the water, turning and returning the wall. As your toddler enters the water spin them by their shoulders to help turn them back towards the wall and encourage them to reach out and grab the wall with their outstretched arms.

It will not take long for this to become their favourite part of their lesson.

BORNTOSWIM.COM.AU ©

Emetsfinn

Horizontal Turns

Horizontal Turns teach your toddler rotation from side to side; an important part of learn to swim and how to roll onto their back unassisted in the event of an accidental fall into the water.

Like Vertical Turns, they should be taught in stages:
- how to submerge and move independently,
- how to float on the back, and
- how to turn horizontally in the water.

To submerge and move independently through the water, practice with your toddler by having them self-submerge and move towards you from a shallow to deeper area in the pool. Hold your arms out to encourage them to reach for you.

Back floating, as previously mentioned entails your toddler being comfortable laying on their back in the water. Little ones who do not like back floating should still be taught to roll onto their back. Assisting and encouraging them should help change their minds.

Turning horizontally requires your toddler to roll from their front onto their back. Kiddies can practice the roll when in bed, in shallow water or on floatation mats. When they practice rolling we want to discourage littlies from lifting their heads, this will cause their legs to drop and their body to feel like it is sinking. Encourage them to stay flat by placing one hand on their chest and one on their back then counting to three and flipping them like a pancake. It becomes a fun game and they will soon learn to do it on their own.

To practice the stages of the Horizontal Turn in succession, we start by calling our toddler into the water from the submerged step using the Conditioning cue. Assist them to turn from their front onto their back by gently grasping their shoulders and rolling them over. Support them with one hand resting under their back and the other supporting their head as they relax into a back float.

As they progress and perfect their Horizontal Turns maintain physical contact by gently holding them by their shoulders until they can manage the turn all by themselves.

Once your toddler has learnt to roll and float onto their back without your assistance, encourage them to kick on their back or roll onto their tummy to kick and paddle to safety.

Safe Exit

Regardless of age, knowing how to exit the water is imperative to water safety. A good rule to insist on is 'if you don't know how you are going to get out, don't go in'.

Climbing out safely starts with learning how to Monkey-Monkey (or crab walk) by gripping firmly onto the pool wall, like a little monkey hanging in a tree, and using a hand-over-hand action to move to a safe place for your toddler to exit.

The Monkey-Monkey will also help build the upper body strength your toddler will need to pull themselves out of the water.

To teach toddlers to climb out, stand behind your tot and have them hold onto the pool wall. Place their hands flat on the pool deck and encourage them to stay close to the wall as they push down with their hands and lift themselves onto their chest then belly using their arms, elbows and feet. Little tots may need your assistance until they can get out without help. To assist, hold them under the armpits as they use their hands, arms, feet and legs. Use the mantra, 'hand-hand, elbow-elbow, belly, feet', so they remember to use their whole body to get themselves out.

That's a wrap!

Swimming uses a lot of energy and acts as a gentle exercise for you and your toddler so be sure to have a healthy snack and towels at the ready when you finish each lesson.

It is also important that any equipment used during the lesson is removed from the pool and surrounding area after use. This is because toys left in the water are a temptation for a small child to reach for and accidentally fall into the water.

By creating a routine and practicing 2-3 times a week, your little one will build a solid foundation of aquatic skills for their Water Awareness Journey.

When you're ready to dive into the next level, check out our 4-Level Learn To Swim The Australian Way Series for kids aged 3 & up where we teach each of the four competitive strokes, water safety, a variety of safe entries, dives and a whole lot more.

Made in the USA
Las Vegas, NV
10 November 2023